Collins

G000242809

BEING ROONEY

Alan Gibbons

CONTENTS

It is Everton v Arsenal. It is Goodison Park in Liverpool. It is 19 October 2002. History is about to be made. The score is 1–1. The game is heading for a draw.

Wayne Rooney is waiting for his chance. He will be seventeen in five days. Wayne gets the call to come off the bench with just ten minutes to go.

Everybody expects Arsenal to see the game out. They are the champions, and they haven't been beaten in thirty games. Surely nothing can stop it becoming thirty-one?

In the ninetieth minute, Wayne brings the ball down thirty metres from goal. He turns, glances up and shifts the ball to his right.

Wayne is too quick for the defender.
His shot flies over the gloves of England legend,
Arsenal keeper David Seaman.
The crowd roars. He is the
youngest goal scorer in
Premier League history!

The commentator salutes
the new star: *"Remember this
name – Wayne Rooney."*

EARLY DAYS

So where did he come from, Wayne Rooney, the boy wonder?

He was born on 24 October 1985, in north Liverpool. His family were mad Everton fans. Football is in his blood. Above is a picture of Wayne when he was just six months old, ready for his first match.

He wasn't the first sportsman in his family. His dad was a boxer. Another relative played semi-professional football.

Wayne's dad is on the left.

Wayne grew up on a tough estate, but he doesn't remember it like that. He had one or two fights as he grew up, but most of the time he kept out of trouble. His mum let him know if she thought he was doing something wrong. He had a happy childhood with loving parents.

"The best thing about our house was that at the back was a youth club with a five-a-side football pitch. I loved climbing over our back fence to play on it."

Wayne went to his first Everton match when he was six months old. Of course Wayne doesn't remember much about it! In early family photos he is almost always wearing his Everton kit. No wonder he grew up football mad.

He started playing in a kids' league when he was seven and scored the winning goal in his first match. It was a taste of things to come.

▲ *Wayne on his second birthday*

▼ *The Copplehouse Boys' team. Can you spot Wayne?*

Everton's bitter rivals, Liverpool Football Club, were interested in Wayne when he was nine. He turned up at their training ground in his Everton shirt! Then the Everton scout invited him to a trial. For Everton-mad Wayne, there was no contest.

Everton asked Wayne's dad if he could sign schoolboy forms. Wayne ran home to tell his mum. She burst into tears!

Wayne and his two younger brothers Graeme (middle) and John (left) in their Everton kits

THE UNDER-10S

Wayne started with Everton when he was nine. There were training sessions three evenings a week. On Sunday mornings, Wayne's team played another Under-10 side from the North West.

One of his early reports says: "the best natural goalscorer I've seen." His dad kept a record of all Wayne's games. Opposite, you can see his record for the first season. Wayne scored 114 goals.

Wayne lived for football. His most memorable game was when the Everton kids beat the Manchester United kids 12–2. He scored an overhead kick from the edge of the box. It was such a special goal, all the parents started clapping, even the Manchester United mums and dads. Wayne was a true blue Everton fan. Little did he guess that one day he would play for United.

"...the best natural goalscorer I've seen..."

TEAM MASCOT

When he was ten, Wayne was the Everton mascot in a derby match with Liverpool. He was allowed to shoot at the goal before the game started. He chipped the club's keeper, Neville Southall, and the ball went into the net. Southall wasn't happy at being beaten by a ten-year-old kid!

> *"I'm a striker. I want to practise striking."*

Time was made at training for the boys to do their homework. Wayne always said he didn't have any!

The next problem was when the coach told Wayne he had to do some defending. It didn't go down well.

"I'm a striker," he said. "I want to practise striking."

The coach told him he wasn't going to play the following Sunday. Wayne went home and told his mum he wasn't going to training any more.

In the end, Wayne's dad told him the coach knew what he was doing. If he wanted to be a footballer, he had to put up with it.

When he was fourteen, Wayne started having problems with his temper. If he made a mistake, he would throw himself into rash tackles. If a defender started to knock him around, he sometimes lashed out against his opponent.

There were no red cards in these matches, so the team manager would take him off. That just made Wayne's temper worse. His will to win was boiling over.

About that time, a teacher took his football from him for bouncing it on the way into a Science lesson. Wayne booted a wall in frustration.

Wayne and his two brothers with Wayne's childhood hero, Duncan Ferguson, who played for Everton

When the school sent for his mum and dad, Wayne insisted he didn't do it. There was one problem: his shoes still had plaster on them from the wall! The school suspended him for two days. He had to work on his temper before it affected his football.

Then, when he was fifteen, his school let him have three days off a week, to train full-time at Everton. The dream of becoming a professional footballer was starting to look more real.

ENGLAND CALL-UP

Wayne's first England call-up came in 2000, for the Under-15s against Wales. He only got on the pitch for the last half-hour, but he was still made Man of the Match.

Altogether, Wayne turned out six times for the England Under-15s. His form for Everton was good, too, as he scored in every round of Everton's FA Youth Cup run.

At the Final, he pulled up his shirt to show a T-shirt with the slogan: "Once a Blue, always a Blue".

At the end of the game, Wayne was named Player of the Final. After the match, the manager said he would be playing with the first team.

Clubs started to ask if Wayne was for sale. He was getting noticed.

To show his commitment to Everton, he signed for the club at the match against Derby County in 2001 and went out onto the pitch in front of 38 000 fans.

Wayne signs a pre-contract with Everton. Young players are not able to sign a full contract until they are 18.

FIRST-TEAM DEBUT

"Rooney! Rooney!"

What a way to make your first-team debut, going onto the pitch to loud chants from the Everton fans! It was 17 August 2002, Everton against Spurs. Wayne went to bed at ten o'clock the night before, but he couldn't sleep … or eat breakfast the next morning.

He walked onto the pitch to the famous Everton anthem, the *Z Cars* theme.

This was it.

Wayne was finding it hard to shut out the chants of "Rooney!". He played behind the main striker, Kevin Campbell. In a small sign of things to come, he set up the opening goal, scored by Mark Pembridge.

Wayne on the attack in the match against Spurs

Wayne came off before the end. He got good reviews for his first match. The game ended 2–2. His professional career was underway.

A PROFESSIONAL WITH EVERTON

The Everton manager said Wayne wouldn't always be in the starting line-up because he was still so young. The team would use him as a sub. It didn't go down well with Wayne. He just wanted to play football.

He scored a couple of goals against Wrexham in the League Cup; then came the famous first Premiership goal against Arsenal.

Wayne Rooney was on his way.

STUNNING STRIKE BY WAYNE ROONEY

Arsenal manager Arsène Wenger described Rooney's goal as "breathtaking" and said that Wayne was "a special talent".

He was voted the BBC's Young Sports Personality of the Year for 2002 while still in his teens.

But he still had a few lessons to learn. At Christmas in 2002, he did a sliding tackle on Birmingham defender Steve Vickers. Vickers needed eight stitches. The ref sent Wayne off. It was his first red card in the Premiership.

PLAYING FOR ENGLAND

In February 2003, Wayne was called up to the England first team. He got his first goal against Macedonia that September.

His half-volley notched up yet another record: at only 17, he was now England's youngest-ever scorer. It wasn't long before he was a key member of the squad, playing in top competitive games.

Wayne scores for England against Macedonia.

Wayne scores his second against Switzerland.

He was in the England squad for Euro 2004, his biggest challenge yet. Things started well. Wayne scored against Switzerland with a header and celebrated with a back flip. In the 75th minute he scored a second: a low, hard shot just inside the post.

By the end of the group stages, he was top scorer in the competition with four goals. England had got through to the quarter-finals!

PROBLEMS

That lined up a match with the hosts Portugal in the quarter-finals. England were 1–0 up when Wayne collided with one of the Portuguese players. His boot came off so he went to get it. When he tried to put the boot back on, he was in pain.

After he limped off, Portugal equalised. They went on to win the penalty shoot-out 6–5. England were out.

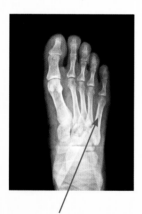

Wayne had broken this bone in his right foot.

There were two reasons for Wayne to be fed up. England were out, and he had a broken bone in his foot.

He was also thinking about his future at Everton. Should he stay or should he go?

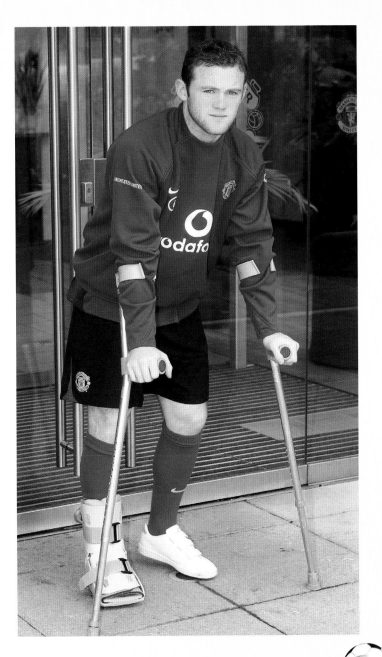

Rumours started that Manchester United wanted to sign Wayne. Everton fans were angry. They remembered him wearing a T-shirt that said "Once a Blue, always a Blue".

Some fans painted the word "Judas" on the wall of his house. There were other signs painted on walls across Liverpool.

Then the news came through. United had offered Everton a huge fee of thirty million pounds to sign him. Everton accepted.

Wayne shows off his new Manchester United shirt, with manager Sir Alex Ferguson.

His first United game was against the Turkish side
Fenerbahçe, in 2004. What a debut it was!

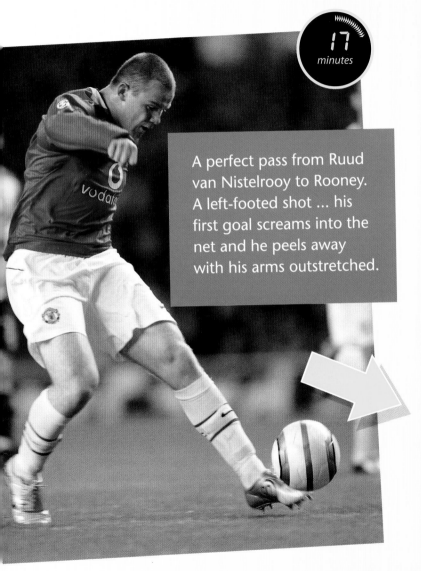

17 minutes

A perfect pass from Ruud
van Nistelrooy to Rooney.
A left-footed shot ... his
first goal screams into the
net and he peels away
with his arms outstretched.

28 minutes

Ryan Giggs puts him through. He dummies the defence, shifts the ball and hits it low across the goal from twenty metres out. Goal number two.

54 minutes

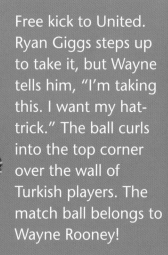

Free kick to United. Ryan Giggs steps up to take it, but Wayne tells him, "I'm taking this. I want my hat-trick." The ball curls into the top corner over the wall of Turkish players. The match ball belongs to Wayne Rooney!

Wayne's first Premiership game was memorable too, but for a different reason. United v Arsenal had been a grudge match for years. United won this one through a late penalty scored by Wayne.

Things got heated between the teams later. There was some pushing and shoving in the tunnel. Somebody threw a slice of pizza and it hit United manager, Sir Alex Ferguson. The press loved the story. They called it "The Battle of the Buffet"!

DIARY OF A TRAINING DAY...

7.15am: Get up!

8.30am: Leave home in Cheshire. Half-hour drive to United's training ground.

9.00am: Change into training kit. Tea and toast in the canteen.

10.00am: Into the gym. Fifteen minutes on the bikes.

10.15am: Boots on and out onto the pitch.

Box work. Passing the ball in the box while other players try to intercept the pass.

10.30am: Tactics. Thirty minutes heading, shooting and crossing.

11.00am: Practice game.

Finish with body work in the gym.

Lunch at the club, then charity or sponsorship work.

4.00pm: rest

...AND A HOME MATCH DAY

Arrive at Old Trafford three hours before kick off.

Meal: spaghetti bolognese with a piece of chicken fillet. Water. Maybe a cup of coffee.

Into the players' lounge.

Short videos of opponents.

Team meeting in the dressing room. Fifteen minutes.

The Boss reads out the team sheet.

Go to the dressing room. Get changed.

Win!

FIRST TROPHY...

Wayne's first trophy for United came in 2006.

It was in the Carling Cup Final against Wigan.

He opened the scoring, driving and hitting the ball

low into the right-hand side of the goal. 1–0!

United strikers Louis Saha and Cristiano Ronaldo

hit two more, but Wayne wasn't finished yet.

He scored a late goal to make it 4–0.

Wayne was voted Man of the Match.

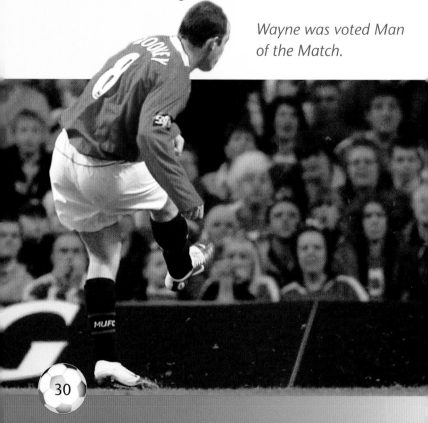

... AND A RED CARD

After recovering from another foot injury,
Wayne was in the 2006 World Cup squad.
England got through to the quarter-finals where
they would meet Portugal. This meant Wayne
would be playing against United team-mate
Cristiano Ronaldo.

It was 0–0 at half time. Eighteen minutes into the second half, Wayne picked up the ball. Three Portuguese players surrounded him. There was a lot of pushing and shoving ... Wayne twisted and turned, fighting for the ball. This is what he said in his book *The Way It Is*:

> *"I lost my balance and landed on the fella on the ground."*

Cristiano Ronaldo ran in. He seemed to want the ref to show a card. Wayne was shocked to see it was red. He was off!

He had to watch the rest of the match in the dressing room.

The match ended 0–0. It was the old England nightmare: penalties.

England missed three of their first four penalties. They were out of the World Cup.

The England lads walked into the changing room. They told Wayne he wasn't to blame. After the match, the England players felt terrible. Their World Cup dream was over.

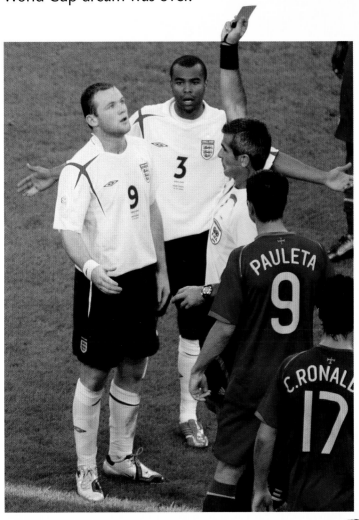

CHAMPIONS LEAGUE WINNER

One of the high points of Wayne's career so far must be the 2008 Champions League Final in Moscow. It was the first all-English final in the competition. United were up against Chelsea.

ALL-ENGLAND FINAL TO CHAMPIONS LEAGUE

And it's Manchester against London, North against South!

Cristiano Ronaldo put United into a 1–0 lead with a header after twenty-six minutes. It was looking good for United.

Then, disaster! In the final minute of the first half, Frank Lampard equalised for Chelsea. The score was 1–1.

Chelsea had United on the back foot in the second half. Extra time was fast and exciting, with Chelsea player Didier Drogba sent off. There were no more goals, which meant a penalty shoot-out.

United won the shoot-out 6–5. Wayne had a Champions League medal.

PREMIERSHIP CHAMPIONS – AND MORE

Great forwards like Ruud van Nistelrooy and Cristiano Ronaldo left United for other clubs. This made Wayne even more important to the team. It needed his hard work, his build-up play and his goals.

By 2013, this was his record with United:

Five Premier League titles

Two League Cups

Three Community Shields

One Champions League Cup

One FIFA Club World Cup

Wayne has won many awards, including Player of the Year, and Goal of the Season three times.

One thing is for sure: it's always exciting when Wayne Rooney is on the pitch!

Wayne holding the Carling Cup (League Cup) in 2006

REACHING FOR THE STARS

This is how Wayne
describes the feeling
of scoring a goal at
Old Trafford:

 Bang!
That feeling kicks in whenever
I score a goal for Manchester
United.
   It takes me over like
nothing else.
   I reckon if I could bottle the
buzz it gives me, I'd make the
best energy drink ever. "

66 Someone's grabbing at my shirt, my heart's banging out of my chest. Then the sound, a roar loud enough to hurt my ears. It's so big, it's right on top of me. And the crowd start singing my name:

"Rooooo-neeee!"

There is no better feeling in the world. 99

66 The buzz of scoring is like nothing else. When it happens, it's like I lose my head. For five or six seconds afterwards I honestly don't know what I'm doing. 99

TWO OF THE BEST

So what are Wayne's best goals? Here are two to think about.

1

Manchester United v Newcastle United
24 April 2005

Wayne hits the ball with the outside of his right foot. The volley bends into the net. Wonder goal.

Manchester United v Manchester City
12 February 2011

This is the famous bicycle kick. Nani crosses the ball. Wayne launches himself into the air and puts the overhead shot past Joe Hart. The keeper does not move. Wayne calls it "the best goal I've scored".

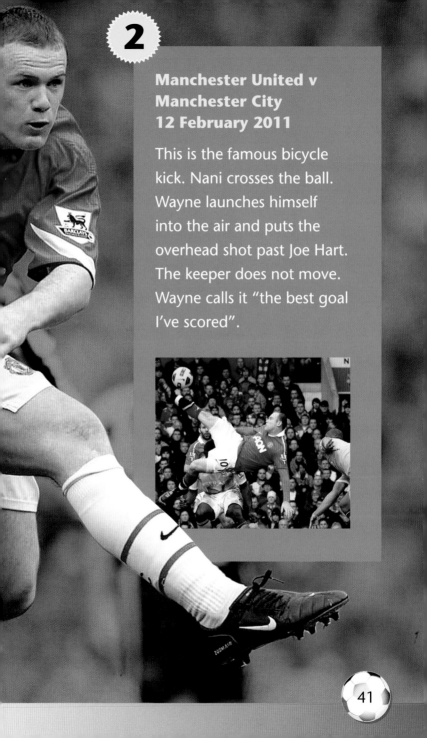

At what age did you believe you could become a pro player?

I joined Everton at nine, but it wasn't until I was about fifteen that I thought I'd make it.

Would you say you have been lucky – or has it been mostly natural ability and hard work?

I would put hard work first, then natural ability – and then luck. I needed luck to break into the Everton team when I did, and then England.

What's the secret of your success?

Some say my eyesight must be amazing, letting me see round corners. Or I must have a swivel head.

I don't think it's either. It's more to do with
painting a picture. Before a ball comes to me,
I look up quickly, taking in where everyone is,
then I won't look up again. Then I pass the ball.
It's done at great speed of course,
so you have to have a good
eye-to-brain connection.
It's come with training
over the years, and with
knowing the players
I'm playing with.

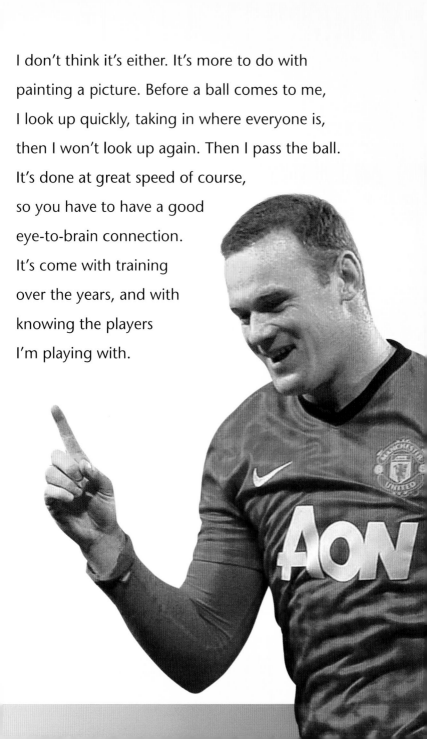

How do you prepare for games?

I always ask the kit man what colour we're wearing – red top, white shorts, white socks or black socks. Then I lie in bed the night before and visualise myself scoring goals.

I don't know if you'd call it visualising or dreaming, but I've always done it, my whole life.

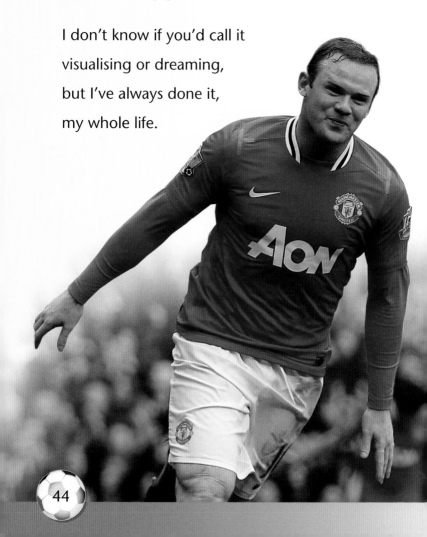

When I was younger, I used to visualise myself scoring wonder goals, stuff like that. From thirty metres out, dribbling through teams. When you're playing professionally, you realise it's important for your preparation.

What do you think is the secret of goalscoring success?

It comes from a combination of coaching and instinct. I practise scoring goals all the time.

I hit volleys.

I hit shots from outside the box.

I hit shots where I have to control a ball passed into my chest.

I hit penalties, free kicks.

But you can't teach instinct. You've either got it or you haven't.

Reader challenge

Word hunt

1 On page 2, find a verb that means "looks briefly".

2 On page 32, find an adjective that means "very surprised".

3 On page 34, find a noun that means "trouble" or "tragedy".

Text sense

4 What happened when Wayne was the Everton mascot? (page 10)

5 What made Wayne lose his temper when he was growing up? (pages 12–13)

6 Why do you think the fans chanted his name when he made his debut for Everton? (page 16)

7 Why did the press call Wayne's first game for United "The Battle of the Buffet"? (page 27)

How do you think Wayne felt when he got sent off in the World Cup quarter-finals? How about his team-mates? (pages 32–33)

Your views

 Which of Wayne's cups and awards do you think means the most to him? Give reasons.

 Did you enjoy the book? Give reasons.

Spell it

With a partner, look at these words and then cover them up.

- debut
- climbing
- knock
- buffet

Take it in turns to read the words aloud. The other person has to try and spell each word. Check your answers, then swap over.

Try it

With a partner, think of three or four questions to ask Rooney and role-play the interview. Find answers to the questions in the text.

William Collins's dream of knowledge for all began with the publication of his first book in 1819. A self-educated mill worker, he not only enriched millions of lives, but also founded a flourishing publishing house. Today, staying true to this spirit, Collins books are packed with inspiration, innovation and practical expertise. They place you at the centre of a world of possibility and give you exactly what you need to explore it.

Collins. Freedom to teach.

Published by Collins Education
An imprint of HarperCollins*Publishers*
77-85 Fulham Palace Road Hammersmith London W6 8JB

Browse the complete Collins Education catalogue at **www.collinseducation.com**

Text by Alan Gibbons ©
HarperCollins*Publishers* Limited 2014

Series consultants: Alan Gibbons and
Natalie Packer

10 9 8 7 6 5 4 3 2 1

ISBN 978-0-00-748894-0

British Library Cataloguing in Publication Data.
A catalogue record for this publication is available from the British Library.

Commissioned by Catherine Martin
Edited by Sue Chapple
Project-managed by Lucy Hobbs and Caroline Green
Proofread by Hugh Hillyard-Parker
Production by Emma Roberts
Design and cover design by Paul Manning

Acknowledgements

The publishers would like to thank the students and teachers of the following schools for their h in trialling the Read On series:

Queensbury School, Queensbury, Bradford
Southfields Academy, London
The English School, Safat, State of Kuwait
Ormiston Six Villages Academy, Chichester

The publishers gratefully acknowledge the permission granted to reproduce the copyright material in this book. While every effort has been made to trace and contact copyright holders, where this has not been possible the publishers will be pleased to make the necessary arrangements at the first opportunity.

The publisher would like to thank the following for permission to reproduce pictures in these pages:

Cover image (c) Alex Livesey/Getty Images

p. 1 Mike Hewitt/Getty Images, p. 3 Mike Egerton/EMPICS Sport/PA, images on pages 4– courtesy of Wayne Rooney, p. 14 Tony Marshall EMPICS Sport, p. 15 Wayne Rooney, p. 17 Clive Brunskill/Getty Images, p. 19 Warren Little/Get Images, p. 20 Laurence Griffiths/Getty Images, p. 21 Ben Radford/Getty Images, p. 22 zirconicusso/Shutterstock, p. 23 Man Utd/Gett Images, p. 24 Man Utd/Getty Images, p. 25 Man Utd/Getty Images, p. 26 Man Utd/Getty Images, p. 27 Man Utd/Getty Images, p. 28 Man Utd/Getty Images, p. 29 Man Utd/Getty Images, p. 30 Jon Super/Press Association Imag p. 33 Bongarts/Getty Images, p. 35 Jamie McDonald/Getty Images, p. 37 Man Utd/Getty Images, p. 38–39 Mike Hewitt/Getty Images, p. 40–41 Jon Super/Press Association Images, p. 43 EPA/Alamy, p. 44 Alex Livesey/Getty Imag